The City
of the
Olesha Fruit

BOOKS BY NORMAN DUBIE

The City
of the
Olesha Fruit

NORMAN DUBIE

DOUBLEDAY & COMPANY, INC.
GARDEN CITY, NEW YORK   1979

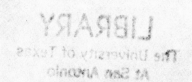

Library of Congress Cataloging in Publication Data

Dubie, Norman, 1945–
  The city of the Olesha fruit.

  I. Title.
PS3554.U255C57   811'.5'4
ISBN: 0-385-14573-X
Library of Congress Catalog Card Number 78-19257

FOR MY BROTHER AND SISTER

If it had not been for the generosity of The John Simon Guggenheim Memorial Foundation I would not have been able to complete this work.

Grateful acknowledgment is made to the following publications in which these poems first appeared:

The American Poetry Review: The Red Fiddle in the Moon Parlor; You; Aubade of the Singer and Saboteur, Marie Triste: 1941; Winter Woods; The Dun Cow and the Hag; Sacrifice of a Virgin in the Mayan Ball Court; a Lamb, a Woolen Lamb; Elegy to the Sioux, and The Seagull.

Antaeus: To Michael; The Black Cloth of the Birdcage Covers the Mirrors of Avignon.

Blue Moon News: The City of the Olesha Fruit.

Field: The Infant.

Grilled Flowers: Thomas Hardy.

Ironwood: After Three Photographs of Brassaï.

Marilyn: Elegy to the Pulley of Superior Oblique.

The Mississippi Review: The Towpath.

The New Yorker: Elizabeth's War with the Christmas Bear: 1601; The Ganges; The Hours, and Norway.

Ploughshares: The Ars Poetica of Søren Kierkegaard.

Porch: A Grandfather's Last Letter.

Yellow Brick Road: A Widow Speaks to the Auroras of a December Night.

Poetry: The Ambassador Diaries of Jean de Bosschère and Edgar Poe.

The Gramercy Review: Winter Mangers, and The Siblings' Woodcut: Dementia Praecox.

Missouri Review: The Great Wall of China.

Some of these poems appeared in two limited-edition volumes: *A Thousand Little Things* (Cummington Press, Abattoir Editions) and *Odalisque in White* (Porch Publications).

NOTES

On page 32, "the pulley of superior oblique" is just part of the musculature of the eye.

You is for Joshua, Jeanne, and Robert. *The Infant* is for Roger Weingarten.

CONTENTS

ONE

THE CITY OF THE OLESHA FRUIT

For Richard

> The spider vanished at the boy's mere
> Desire to touch it with his hand.
>
> YURI OLESHA

Outside the window past the two hills there is the city
Where the color-blind are waking to blue pears;
Also, there are the blue treetops waving
To the schoolgirls who step harshly along
In winter dresses: out of the mouths of these girls
Come the cones, their breath,
A mist like the little silver ear trumpets
Of deaf children tipped toward whatever it is
They are almost hearing.

An old man without legs, not yet in a chair, has
Invented the city outside the window.
And everywhere now it is morning! He hears

His wife climbing the stairs.
What, he thinks . . . what to do?
The strong line of her back
Is like a spoon.
He says, "Good morning and how are you?"
She says, "Rumen,
I told you the hen should have been put
Up with straw in the attic. Last night the fox
Ate all of her but the dark spurs under her chin
And a few feathers."

His wife gathers him up in her arms, walks to the far
Corner of the room and lowers him into a straight chair
Beside a table. Only last year he would sit
And stare at the shoes he could wear, without socks

And with the laces loose.
A tub is filling in another room.

He thinks, poor Widow is inside the stomach
Of a fox. My wife's idea was not a good one:
Where would Widow have found the scratch
And gravel for her shells while up in the attic?
And what about
The rooster! What about the poor rooster
On his railing by the barn; inconsolable, crowing?
Rumen remembers a Russian story about a copper rooster
With a green fern for a tail.
Rumen's favorite writer is the great Russian
Yuri Olesha. Rumen thinks, "Yes, Yuri, my companion,
There is cruelty in the format of a kiss!
And the blue skins of pears
In a heap on a dish leave a memory

Of myself as a boy running along the flume water
Down past the village ditch.
But, Yuri, in my city all the streets are,
Just this moment, being swept: old women
In jade dresses sweeping, sweeping.
And soon it will rain for them and then
I'll return their sun, a noon sun
To take away the wet before the children
Rush out under the bells for an hour's recess.

Oh, Yuri, just beyond the grin of a smelly
Old fox, that's where Widow is, our best hen!
Yuri, my legs, I think, are buried in the orchard
Beside the stable where all the hospital horses
Of my city wait, poised for an emergency.
These horses are constant; how they race
Down the cobbled streets for me. They've never
Trampled the children!"

"Rumen," his wife called, "do you want a haircut
This morning?" She steps into the room.
He smiles at her. She is buttoning her blouse.
And she smiles back to him. Rumen would say

To Yuri that sometimes her yellow hair
Got into the corners of his mouth.
"And, Yuri, that was when I most missed my youth."
Then Rumen would again fall silent.
He was off opening a raincloud over his city.
It was winter when he woke, but now I'm sure it's
Not. There are a few dark flowers?
Rumen feels that it is best for the children
If they walk to school in the clear winter air, but
Once he gets around to raining on his trees,
Streets and houses, well, then he changes everything
To late July or August.
But the evenings in his city are always
Placed in autumn: there is the smell
Of woodsmoke, so pleasant,
And leaves burning. Flocks of bluebirds would be
Flying south.

                          *

And so there is the obscurity of many lives,
Not yours, Olesha, but mine and my wife's,
Two characters
Who are, perhaps, in a shade
Just now sipping an iced summer tea
With its twigs and leaves floating around inside:

We are giggling, I think, about how shy
We were as lovers that first winter night
When I kissed her in the dark barn
Right in her open eye. I tried again
And missed again. To accidently kiss a young girl

In her open eye is, I think,
The beginning of experience. *Yuri,*
I did find her mouth that night!

But then the following winter, a week before
Our wedding, I missed again, this time
I kissed a small bare breast.
That wasn't an accident—

She reached out to touch my hand
And found my thigh!
The shyness of lovers, as softly, at night,
They miss and miss while following an old map, yes,
The format of a kiss.
In the city of the Olesha fruit

A citizen never dies, he just wakes
One morning without his legs, and then he is given
A city of his very own making:

In this way his existence narrows
While expanding like a diary, or
Like this landscape with two hills
Seen through my window early
Each and every winter morning! But, Yuri,
Outside this window—yes, I know,

What's there is there, and all of it
Indelible as our memory of blue pears, washed
And being eaten in the sunlight of a city
That is being constructed all of the time,
Its new gold domes and towers,
Just beyond two hills in the winter air, and
Somewhere inside the mind.

THE HOURS

For Ingrid Erhardt (1951–71)

The meadows are empty. There are two villages:
One to the north and another to the south.
It's first light, and the two villages are striking
Their two bells. This is a green valley
That has an echo. Now, the bell to the south
Follows immediately the bell in the north.
So when the bell to the north is struck
Its echo is not heard by anyone for it is lost
In the sound from the south. A pilgrim
Has just climbed down into the valley.
Does he believe that he hears
One, two or four bells working in the morning?

This much is clear: when the bells stopped
The pilgrim thought, at first, that he had
Heard last that bell to the north, followed
By the bell to the south, followed by the echo
Of the bell to the south. So he would tell us
That there are three bells being struck
In the morning. But
You know how after hearing bells
You seem to carry them around
For some time inside your skull? And, also,
The echo of the bell to the north that is lost
So often each morning, where does it go?

Perhaps, it goes where the pilgrim is going. And
Neither north, nor south. We will all be lost,
Even down to the very last memories that others have
Of us, and then these others who survived us, they

Too will be lost. There were many more bells
Than we thought, they will

Never stop for us, as waking to them we realize that
Throughout our lives, in the light and in the dark,

We were always counting our losses.

SACRIFICE OF A VIRGIN IN THE MAYAN BALL COURT

There are the many red birds holding a document
That is written in red,
Red lettering flocking on the page
And off from it at each corner; each corner is appointed
A single colorless bird, perhaps, drained
Like the virgin beneath it.
This, then, is the ceiling! At the center of the room

There is a priest at a stone table. On the table
There is the girl: a breast hangs smoking on its
Hinge of skin, there's an opening in her chest
And her heart has been carried off on a cold plate.
This little vacancy in the girl's chest is
Like a small pond turning red at sunset, is,
For this society of men dressed in bright feathers,
Their *only* antecedent for true feeling! There is

This red emergency of birds above a priest, and a
Painted confusion of stars at his feet.
Last night, outside Phoenix in the desert, among
The creosote and the flowering agave-plants, the body

Of yet another nude girl was discovered by children.
She had been stabbed repeatedly. The sheriff
Insists that he is looking in West Phoenix
For a middle-aged man, *a psychopath who will seem
Perfectly ordinary to his family and friends.*

Imagine them this past weekend outside Flagstaff
Beside a pond that is turning red at evening,
And, *there,* at the center of the pond standing
In a small boat is the man:

He is hated, he is *wanted*—and
Soon, perhaps, he'll be hunted
In the mountains north of the desert.
In the Mayan Ball Court he was the antecedent
Of all time and space! And isn't he, after all, sick

At heart and in his stomach, while shocked he again walks
Out of the desert staring at his red hands
That are like two red fluttering birds?

He is returning to our world: to
Its religions and its ball courts. Returning, and

To kill. *Again!*

YOU

The sunlight passes through the window into the room
Where you are sewing a button to your blouse: outside
Water in the fountain rises
Toward a cloud. This plume of water is lighter
Now, for white shares of itself are falling back
Toward the ground.
This water does succeed, like us,
In nearing a perfect exhaustion,
Which is its origin. The water

Succeeds in leaving the ground but
It fails at its desire to reach a cloud. It pauses,
Falling back into its blue trough; of course,
Another climb is inevitable, and this loud, falling
Water is a figure for love, not loss, and

Still heavy with its desire to be the cloud.

A WIDOW SPEAKS TO THE AURORAS
OF A DECEMBER NIGHT

My yard with its pines is almost spherical in winter.

The green awning outside the window is torn
By heavy snow. I sit in the cane chair.
Beside me, within reach, the gramophone grinds out
A little Debussy: the horn
Of the gramophone is plugged with a sock.

An artery stands out at my ankle
And these little crossings
Of blood do blossom secretly in the leg, climbing
Up to the heart or lungs. There's the
Familiar light coming on in the distance in the dark city:

It has been a spark within a house above my pines
Before sunrise each winter for these
Past three years of just tea and the *Times*.
I often remember
An especially dry gin from the barroom
At the Ritz Tower. The watercolor my husband purchased
In Caracas remains in the corner
Bound in twine, and dark caramel papers; it has a
Big postage stamp depicting a native girl
Holding up a blue turtle.

The familiar light above the pines goes out. A man
Has dipped both of his hands into a stream of cold water.
He has washed his teeth and hair. Clean-shaven,
He greets his wife in their kitchen. She has fried
Some trout with bacon. Outside my window the sapphire light
Of the northeast-Packet plane lifts up out of Hartford,

Its soft, watery light dips and then
Leans into a sunrise:
There is snow, pines and two sheep who have wandered
From a neighbor's farm beyond the Reservoir—
Just this winter scene, and two wide sheep that
Are the blue-white of a chunk of fat

Falling off the dangerous, true edge of daylight.

AFTER THREE PHOTOGRAPHS
OF BRASSAÏ

A whore moves a basin of green antiseptic water
Away from the towels to a clean white shelf.
A Russian sailor rests against the wall smelling
Of tobacco.

The tall narrow mirror has little dark flecks
Within it like the black sinks of a smoky, surgical theater
Seen from the balconies: the whore
From *above* is now below us, in the future, on a table where

Two students in white gowns are struggling to open her:
The ribs cracking back, the pink gill-like trench
Follows the thin hairline down the center
Of her stomach to where the knife shallows on pelvic bone.

A student beside us vomits and his breakfast of warm milk
Falls slowly to the floor passing tier after tier
Of first year students. The autopsy is over.
The charwoman in a yellow bonnet is mopping up.

And the same dead girl is now, again, moving the green water
Away from the soiled towels. A banker
Smelling of jasmine is dressing himself. The whore straightens
Her shoulders, this girl who is always bent

Over herself. Her fingers which she chews are hurt
By an acid douche. She straightens her shoulders
As she stares into a black speck in the mirror so as
To forget. She begins singing, also, to forget;

The banker stepping into his taxi is trying to remember
If there was a mole on her neck, if this one's name

Was Claudette? And he is stepping into the taxi, he is
Drunk and falling into the blackness of it: his shoe flies

Up into the night as high as the colored numerals and lights.
The door slams shut. The charwoman has finished mopping up,
She turns out the lights. You are now alone in the upper-
Most balcony looking down for a floor through the darkness.

You drop a pencil waiting to hear it strike the boards . . .
It falls stiff like a drunk, like a drunk falling onto a whore.

THE GANGES

I'm sorry but we can't go to the immersions tonight
For the poor will not get down from the wheel, and
The musicians and the lorry won't budge
Without the money. We don't have it. But, we could

Walk to the cremations. It will be dark with a mist
Where the stairs jump into the water. These are
The funeral ghats. The corpses are brought in drapes
And that one will be dipped in the river and then
She will be anointed with clarified butter. To the
Left of us four men waist deep in the river sift
Through mud and ashes for gold rings.
With a straw torch
The dead mother's son starts the fire;
With a bone cudgel
He smashes her skull to release the images shared
By her with these

Postcards I am now passing to you:
Of the family pond entirely filled with limes,
White pigs rooting in coconut husks, and her six
Children watering their charges, the black lulled elephants.

THE TOWPATH

Two mules being led by a black silhouette
Along the steamy morning's path
Of oak and spotted sorrel hedge:

The silhouette, almost a boy's figure,
Walking between the heads of mules,
Is missing an arm and part of a shoulder;

This ghost, this cripple in the late
Morning mist, seen from the canal, seen from the boat
The mules are towing, is

A lie—just a cloud of angry deerflies!
At noon, they'll stop for cold pork on bread.
The boatman's wife will slap mud on the backs

Of the mules. Put straw hats on their heads.
Water them. And give
Them timothy and sugar from her open hands.

The mules lean into the rope again
Eating as they go the dry yellow spears of colic-root,
The only thing that grows on the towpath.

The towpath is a hard, blue clay with, here and
There, the fresh droppings of these animals.
If the tow-rope broke the mules would

Fall painfully forward! If a leg of a mule was broken,
A black and silver Winchester would come out
Of the powder-closet. To bury

A mule in a shallow grave you must
Break its three remaining legs!
If you are Irish you stick a red flag

In the mound so that your countrymen
Who are starving out in the woods, fugitive
And dying of smallpox, will understand

That here there is fresh red meat for the children.
You signal them to come with two
Slow tugs on the big copper bells . . .

Later, at dusk, a breeze comes to your back
And your wife raises the iron clew with the heavily patched sail.
You drop the plank and then walk the mule

Down to the cellar of the boat where it eats
Oats and bran,
Where it eats a soft apple from your wife's hand . . .

But does this beast standing inside under a moving lamp,
Standing in dark steerage with goats and potatoes,
Desire this circumstance, on water, pushed by a breeze?

Doesn't the mule want to be outside in the real dark
And at the true center of his burden
On a blue clay path with sparks of colic-root

Beneath him; free
To drag everything along behind him
Under the old, the very old, and sulking trees?

THE INFANT

> There are possibilities for me, but under
> What stone, Father, do they lie?
>
> KAFKA

Franz, under what stone. *You ask me under what stone?*
Knowing you, I would say—under *your* gravestone, in Prague.

You say that you can't write and yet at night you scribble
Until the light. You use paper like the successful bureaucrat

That you are. Vice Secretary of the Workers' Accident
Institute. And yet you insist that there is nothing

In this world you can do. You hate the grandchildren,
Their noises frighten you.

You write poor Felice and say that now you are in love
With another. It was a perfect setting for a romance,

The sanatorium in Riva! After troubling Felice with a rival,
And in the very same letter, you suddenly tell her

That you are on your knees, and will *she* be your wife?
You hurt her with silence. You hurt her when you write.

Martin Buber bores you.
Oklahoma bores you. Moses bores you.

Dead flowers on your desk excite you.
Rain excites you. And your sister's lacerated leg is all you'll

Hear of at the breakfast table!
Grete Bloch insists that we should grant your wish to live

In the woods with ghosts. Go then, will you? I'll throw the
Latch back on the door myself for you. I'll carry you

To the woods. You love to lie on your mother's sofa
With a headache. When your sister bakes, you wait for her

Shout, and then you run down to us in glee to see a burn
Wrapped in stinging leaves.

Under stones, indeed; with the snakes, worms and darning-fleas.
Yes, even for you there are possibilities.

Your disease is your desire
Not to be.

In the mousy darkness only the thought of cows
Keeps you from madness.

Your mother wishes you would help us with the coal bill.
I laughed. The truck driver laughed.

I look back to ask what I did wrong. What I hear
Is myself with you in my arms. When you were a baby

In your long gray gowns I sang to you the best songs.
I loved the one about the three-legged mule. And the

One where a giant sat on a toadstool.
You love the cat.

You watch it at its milk and then
Follow it to its box of sand. She arches her back.

And you make notes. You write that, at that moment, you have
No worries. What that vicious cat leaves in its box

You place in your novels—the undigested bones and tails
Of mice.

You, at your job, are so cold to the husky laborer who
Has a broken arm. But let the debtor, pensioner, whore

Come sobbing to you and you in tears respond, "Oh, isn't
It awful what happens to the weak and wronged."

You say that you can't deplore your selfishness, your
Silence, hypochondria and tears, for they're the reflection

Of a higher consciousness that is impossible to understand.
To fear! *Franz,*

Don't lie. It's not under your gravestone that the possibilities
Lie, but here under mine. *And I survived you!*

Your mother and I today visited
Your grave at Strašnice. There was a black little acre

Beyond your grave off in the distance. Probably a potato field?
I made these words!

I'm not ashamed. *I will go off to eat*
A large sandwich. Then, I will wash my feet.

WINTER MANGERS

Sheep are flooding like turning muddy water
Down out of the south gate onto the road where snow
Is banked high into the night
Touching the lowered branches of oaks.

A sleigh rounds the corner into
An encounter with a black ewe
Who turns in fright, chips of ice shooting
Back from her hooves.

The sleigh has stopped for the sheep
Who are being whistled through the north gate
To mangers that are scattered to the side
Of the brick farmhouse.

From in back of the barn a leaping
Rouen duck has lost her purple
And white crown which feathered its way
Down to a lump on her neck—*just where
The axe sunk into the tree stump!*
The confounded duck leaps once more with a wing outstretched,
Weighted with blood . . .
Out in the field a scarecrow steps
Into moonlight.

The reins of the sleigh rise, then straighten
On the horse's rump and raw shoulders.
The snow begins to drift a little. The fat ewe
Looks over herself at the faded weathervane
Of the abattoir: inside

The washed stone gutters descend
From an elevated floor—black with the old blood
Of slaughter.
The moving sleigh is like a painted iron swan in a carnival's

Shooting gallery. There is the distant prattle of sleigh bells,
And until the trees began to swarm, at sunset, the tall farmer
And his wife and children were all
In the barnyard to be viewed by anyone. But with the coming
Of moonlight they are all suddenly absent.

At this hour they have lost dominion over the animals
And they will soon be naked and solitary like the black ewe
Who is huddled inside a straw-filled manger, looking out
Beyond the slaughterhouse

To the scarecrow who wanders like a broken prince
Across the icy, rose-madder darkness, wanders
That is, until cockcrow
Returns his blue rags, and the day begins to collect
Its taxes in the inert sunshine of this Kingdom . . .

TWO

THE DUN COW AND THE HAG

Beside the river Volga near the village of Anskijkovka
On a bright summer day

An old woman sat sewing
By the riverbank. If asked she would say

She was lowering the hem of a black dress.
All while she sewed

A cow stood beside her. They were ignored
As the day passed; by evening, a merchant

From Novgorod arrived with his family
At the riverbank carrying baskets,

And his eldest daughter down beyond a clump
Of white birches undressed and stepped

Into the river, the girl's breasts
Are large and moved separately like twins

Handed from one serf to the next
Down to a river for baptism. The merchant,

His wife, and their son are seated
In the grass eating chunks of pink fish

That they dip in scented butter. The fish
Spoiled as it rode in the sun on the top

Of their carriage. These three have been poisoned
And can be seen kneeling in the grass.

The daughter who was bathing in the river
Is, now, crying for anyone to help her: the hag

Leaves her cow to walk down to the floundering girl:
Just her arms above the water

Working like scissors.
She cut the thread for the old woman.

It was summertime on the river Volga, and the old woman
Told the cow

That this could happen to anyone and that
It *had* happened once to them; and

It was summertime on the river Volga,
The black water

Ran off her dress like a lowered hem.

A GRANDFATHER'S LAST LETTER

For Hannah

Elise, I have your valentine with the red shoes. I have
Waited too many weeks to write—wanting to describe
The excitement on the back lawn for you:
                                        the forsythia

Is now a bright yellow, and with the ribbons you draped
Inside it, trembles in a breeze,
All yellow and blues, like that pilot light this winter
Worried by just a little breath that came out of you.

On the dark side of the barn there's the usual railing
Of snow.
The tawny owl, nightingales and moles
Have all returned to the lawn again.

I have closed your grandmother's front rooms.

I know you miss her too. Her crocus bed showed its first
Green nose this morning. For breakfast I had
A duck's egg and muffins.

Your father thinks I shouldn't be alone?
Tell him I have planted a row of volunteer radishes.
I have replaced the north window . . .

So you have read your first book. Sewed a dress for
The doll. The very young and old are best at finding
Little things to do. The world is jealous of us, you know?

The moles are busy too. Much more mature this year,
The boar with the black velvet coat made a twelve
Foot long gallery under the linden where the mockingbirds
Are nesting.

The moles took some of my rags to add to
Their nursery of grass, leaves and roots.
The cream-colored sow is yet to make her appearance!
They have seven mounds. Each with three bolt doors
Or holes.
The pine martens are down from the woods, I see them
In the moonlight waiting for a kill.

Molehills can weaken a field so that a train
Passing through it sinks suddenly, the sleepers
In their berths sinking too!

I wonder what it's like in their underground rooms:
Their whiskers telegraphing the movements
Of earthworms. They don't require water when on
A steady diet of nightcrawlers. Worms are almost
Entirely made of water.

Last night there was quite an incident. The sun was going
Down and the silly boar was tunneling toward
The linden and he went shallow, the owl dropped down
Setting its claws into the lawn, actually taking hold
Of the blind mole, at that moment the mockingbird
Thinking her nest threatened fell on the owl putting
Her tiny talons into the shoulders of the owl. Well,

There they were, Elise, the owl on top of the invisible
Mole, the mockingbird on top of the owl. The mole
Moved backwards a foot,
The birds were helpless and moved with him.
They formed quite a totem. The two birds looked so serious
In their predicament. A wind brushed the wash on the line.
And our three friends broke each for its respective zone.

Tomorrow the vines on the house are coming down. I want
The warmth of the sun on that wall. I'm sending

You a package with some of your grandmother's old clay
Dolls, silverware and doilies.

Tell your father he is not coming in June to kill
The moles! Tell him to go fishing instead, or to take
Your mother to Florida.

You said you worry that someday I'll be dead also! Well,
Elise, of course, I will. I'll be hiding then from your world
Just like our moles. They move through their tunnels
With a swimming motion. They don't know where they're
                                  going—
But they go.

There's more to this life than we know. If ever
You're sleeping in a train on the northern prairies
And everything sinks a little
But keeps on going, then, you've visited me in another world—

Where I am going.

ELEGY TO THE PULLEY OF SUPERIOR OBLIQUE

Weston's photograph of a border bridge

The three girls in a donkey cart are
Ascending the tiled adobe bridge, its little arc
Over the dry wash under a noonday sun. Below them
A wizened farmer with a bag of grain sleeps in the shadows
Of the bridge while sitting on the dry river
Bottom which looks like a long black skid mark
Vanishing off the side of a cliff on the highway beyond
The purple mountains.

There are miserable people, standing for the duration
In a halated light, whom I would never describe

For it would be a lie. To write, for example, that
Two house flies are like two fiddles drying
In a mahogany vise beside
The blue chisels and almond pastes; that all over the shop
Fans are blowing across the huge blocks of ice.
That would be a lie! There's blood on an apron and
The green checkered bills in the cigar box. And
The carpenter's wife is a Jew. This is Warsaw ten years
Before my birth. The sweltering ghetto! Months later,
The sweltering snow!

So I must tell you that the sisters in the cart are
Unhappy and not beautiful. They have suffered scabs and
Diarrhea. They have boiled water out in their yard,
Beside the deep, fragrant cilia plants, and had been too weak
To drag the scalded water just a foot or two beyond the fire.
They have all fainted, once or twice,
While squatting in the trench out behind their barn.
This influenza killed their mother. And aunt.

And, now, they have crossed the bridge and the donkey
Looks under his belly; slumps to one side, and falls
Dead.
The younger sister begins to sob.
The oldest jumps from the cart and runs down a pebble slope
To the sleeping farmer.
The farmer wakes, frightened, not for a moment looking
Away from the girl's chest that is running with sores.
He says, "A man is taking our picture from above!"
The toothless farmer then waves to Weston, and
The girl slumps onto the brown river bed with her arms
Around herself.
There are dogs sniffing near the donkey.
There are two flies. And

What does this sick girl have to do with
Our lives? That excellent man, *Rosen,* knows:

Open your eyes: there's sky, mountains; the moment
Of death is instant, contrived.

NORWAY

For Elizabeth Paũs

The raw slopes of meat are stabbed with pikes
And the flesh of the whale is torn away
With the use of hands and feet. Here and there
A gull cries. This fish turned to oil, the oil turning
To a carbon band around the chimney of a crystal lamp,

And, at midnight, a man closes his book. He sighs,
Closes his eyes,
And, then, it is there in the purple haze of his mind
That the whale leaps
For a last time; dancing a little, just an element
Of white oval light in a lamp.
It had spread past the seated man,
Past the table at his right hand to a sleeping dog,
But it failed at touching the far corner
Of the room—its tiny vase of blue and black pansies stands

With the smudged faces of exhausted whalers,
Their red arms stirring the big iron pots while
Above them on the deck a cabin boy leans on a broom,
Stopped at his work, his mouth open: he just gazes
At a brain of a whale
That is steaming like a newborn calf outside
In the early spring rain that has turned to hail.

TO MICHAEL

Petrarch must have known why we and the goldfinch
Can't sleep. He sat below a twisted pear tree mourning
A woman while two blackbirds ate at his open sleeves.
He is inside Avignon on a bench beside the fountains
Where two elderly men swing sulphur-and-tar pots
As they sing. The sharp

Disinfectant in their pots reaches this man seated in a breeze;
And the plague is in all the cities to the north!
He has an image of a woman climbing through a field.
Laura has been dead of cholera for two weeks.
He speaks to the two blackbirds, now ascending

Into the pear tree, "Little things, a gift of paper.
The sulphur-and-tar pots, their fat blossoms
Swinging on the curve like sun spots
On the blade of an axe lifted into the blue sky
And, then, dropped like sudden rain into the valley:
Two stooped figures running away from the scaffolding

With a heavy basket; freshly washed, yellow hair
Spilling over the sides of the basket!
Lives are being ended everywhere. Laura died.
Sitting in her bed, two servants held a mirror
For her, the two women were weeping: she stared
At her forehead—

At the red pits that are plugged with the stinging gum
From cedars. They lowered the corpse into a boiling tub
Along with the heads of daffodils and roses." And so, Michael,
I think he must have known
There in the sunlight, in Avignon, that rain would enter
The valley drowning all the steep burial-fires,

The sulphur-and-tar pots smoking—a baker
Lifts his white apron and runs through a doorway!
Petrarch still sits under the pear tree in the rain
Watching the water in the fountains fight to climb
Through water that is emptying down all around them;
The invisible is now visible here:

The sickness is presented
By the mere absence of people in the rain
As water spills from the troughs of the fountains
Onto the streets, reaching the feet of a man
Seated below a pear tree. You can see
Tears plummeting from the high bones of his cheeks.

THE SEAGULL

Chekov, at Yalta

A winter evening at the cottage by the bay,
And I sat in the black and gold of the dead garden
Wrapped in blankets, eating my sister's suet pudding.
The fountain was wrapped in a dirty straw and

Just below my property in the old Tartar cemetery
There is a small funeral in progress: the widow
Is wearing a purple shawl, the children are bare around
The shoulders and the girls are wearing orange petals

At their throats. The ashen white beards of the men
Are like immaculate vests from this distance.
There is nothing more intolerable than suet pudding,
Unless it is the visitors. The drunken visitors laughing

In my kitchen, eating my duck and venison, while I hide
From them here in the dark garden.
The daughter of one of these gentlemen is pretty.
I saw her through the window drinking

Champagne from a clay mug—just under her thin blouse
I saw the blue points of her breasts that turn,
In opposition, both out and up like the azure slippers
Of the priest who is now singing in the cemetery below my
                                                    house.

Once the family has gone off with its torches I'll
Climb down to the fresh grave and drop some coins
For flowers, for sweets for the children, and
Perhaps, even wooden teeth for the widow so she can

Attract a new husband? The black, turned soil
Of our garden reminds me
Of the common grave given to the children
Of the Godunov Orphanage after that horrible fire:

A charred horse was thrown in with them,
Bags of lime and what I understood to be a large ham
That the authorities, nevertheless, declared
The torso of a male child of nine or ten. The Czar,

In their memory, placed a tiny trout pond over them
And this inscription: *A blue blanket for my little ones.*
My wife goes nearly naked to parties in Moscow.
My sister here, at Yalta, goes sea bathing with a rope

Around her that runs back to the beach where it is
Attached to a donkey who is commanded by a servant
With a long switch.
The sea tows her out and then the donkey is whipped

Sorrowfully until he has dragged her back to them.
I named the donkey, Moon, after the mystery of his service
To my sister. This winter
He has been an excellent friend.

I read to this poor beast from *Three Sisters.* He is a better
Critic and audience than I could find in the cities.
I have won an Award that will save me from arrest anywhere
Inside Russia. I am going to refuse it! And then travel

To Nice or Paris.
My tuberculosis is worse. Tolstoy reads my stories
To his family after supper. And reads them badly, I suppose!
I did walk that evening all the way down to the cemetery

Only to discover that my pockets were empty.
I screamed up to the house for coins, for plenty
Of coins! The visitors, laughing and singing, ran down
To me without coats and with a lantern swinging—

My sister trailed behind them
On her donkey. Her square black hat
Bobbing like a steamer way out in the bay.
And when they reached me—

I said, "Sister, pack the trunks! You hurt me!
I will write that we have departed for France, for Italy."

THE OLD ASYLUM OF THE NARRAGANSETTS

A dark Pilgrim couple in white bibs walks along a barricade of
                  logs
To the blockhouse within which
Two cloaked figures, in candlelight, stand and study
Mistress Sheffield's goose, nailed to the narrow door
By clergy. John Sheffield's children, at dusk,
Struggle through the snow carrying two baskets of honey
                  calabash.

There's a fire beside the old saltboxes of the Waterfront,
A wood smoke with the nauseous, weighted odor
Of night-flowering phlox. Below the piers, the Atlantic

Sleeps in the sheltered harbor.

The Magistrate's dogs are running a deer out across
The saltmarsh. On Burial Hill fresh graves are ignited
With dropped bundles of poinsettia, and here a Pilgrim
Nests like a page of testament, bound
By abundant scripture. The small Plymouth choir
In red shawls scatters voices along
The street, down around the corner
To the Governor's gabled house where in the upper window
Candles are moving in a sickroom—

The Governor's niece has contracted cholera!

The pious physician sits in a chair and eats steadily from
A plate of Mistress Blaisdale's caramel divinity, peppermints
And marchpane. At morning, he'll find the sick girl
Sitting under her cap,
Eyes open—with fever broken; hours later from the balcony,
The Governor with arms extended above the wilderness
Sings his proclamation of joy, and,

This early November morning, the treetops on the hill
Are inky with intervals of opalescent sky
That's fired by the sunrise. The shadows along the Waterfront
Will expel an Indian in a dugout,
A still warm doe roped around his neck and shoulders;

The lowing cows wear bells of brass and antimony,

Their silhouettes across the pasture of the Common
Are like small bobbing ships, processional
And violet in the wintry canals
Of Holland . . . the witch, Mistress Sheffield,
Is in her coffin, the creamy marl

Of her hands at her neck,
The dagger drinking there: a dragonfly beaded with amethyst,
Its wings beating invisibly
Like the cold puritan heart exalted above its wilderness.

THREE

THE AMBASSADOR DIARIES OF JEAN DE BOSSCHÈRE AND EDGAR POE

For Michael Burkard

> The house of evening, the house of clouds, vast hall
> of which the walls are walls of everywhere.
>
> *
>
> Pitiful child, pitiful crystal,
> with your four o'clocks and half-past threes,
> your fingernails; *their* wounds, your simple disbelief,
> your glass of water and your wine and mirrors,
> english for poetry, french for prose,
> your books, your box of letters—*love and believe them,*
>
> since so you must, poor victim of the curve,
> collect your odds and ends, and build!
>
> CONRAD AIKEN

I would like to see you in the morning
Before the day's begun. I promised you the jonquils!
You would say, pointing with your giant finger:
There, that's purple-hyssop, and next
To it, cornflowers, phlox and a toad.
Down under the sycamores I would say:

This is where the King's deer stand at night
To dream, and during the day the King's mules,
Roped to pleasure-barges, graze along the riverbanks,
And everywhere, here, there are
The droppings of deer and mules, all
Up and down the Thames, its streams and canals—

Canals like halls, the high tents of sycamores that Tse-tse
adored.
And Henry VIII, you wrote,
Stood up in a tower: wine, potato
And pink wild-pig in his beard, and the rain
Outside his window was like a curtain
Being drawn in Asia by

A dark courtesan with long, white braids.
King Henry flung his cup out the turret window
And it struck a rock, bouncing back up, then,
Falling through the wet lilac; at last, resting
In the meadow where in the rain three cows
Are lying down. *Your King, like us, is sane.*

Isn't he? Aren't you . . . A.,
An hour later we see him descending
The turret stairs. I think we fear this man?
As he goes down to the meadow through the rain.
He's drunk and curses the weather, his mother,
His mother's mother. He's searching

For the silver cup. He peers into bushes.
He sweeps his long, blue slipper through
The grass.
His yellow sleeves are dripping wet as he stumbles
Past lilac into the meadow. He kneels,
And lifts the cup, tipping

It to his mouth to drink some
Rainwater. A slobbering, steaming cow looks up
With melancholy at young King Henry VIII who looks
Away toward the checkered towers of his castle.
He, then, stares straight back at the cow
With its downcast eyes. The King says, "Damn!"

He lies down with the cows
To sleep. Servants are falling along the
Hillside to aid him, to bring
Henry inside where two girls and his mother
Are waiting with dry linens. Dear A., we
Did guess the meaning of your King! His quest,

A joke about our need to be down there
In the muddy fields, dreaming
Of a glistening castle above us
In the remote, blue air.
You saw, through a window, your father grab
Your mother. You said, to your astonished dolls,

"My father's shot my mother."
You were never sure who struggled more in that
Dark room that morning:
Your father paused, while dressing, to murder
Your mother, to murder *your* father!
Out in the gardens in the dollhouse,

Your knife beside the strawberries and bread,
You watched them, as from a hill.
You pushed open with your hands
And forehead the mahogany door. You stood!
You laid your head between them. It begins to rain.
There was a voice speaking:

*It's only a handkerchief—see? Dear,
I've gotten a flower. Honest, I didn't know.* Earlier,
Your mother had washed your legs. Brushed your hair.
Then . . . just wide-eyed dolls, red-eyed dolls
In your cedar dollhouse—of which the walls
Are walls of terror, everywhere, beside bone-dry jonquils.

*

—*idyll*

Goya who drew a pig on a wall. Goya who drew
Four slatterns in an attic. Goya who etched
A lily on a leaf and threw the leaf back
Into the other leaves of a larger world. Goya who

Wore out the elbows of his sleeves. Jean de Bosschère
Once robbed a merchant. Found 21 ways of describing

A bluebird in snow. Cut his own hair on alternate
Wednesdays.
Goya said, "Why wake the ones who sleep, if awake they
Can only weep." Well, so much for the next world.
The next week! (The princes and priests wanted to pickle
His feet.)

Now think: what comes after Wednesday—for the old woman
Dressed in white across the street who fell down this morning,
Which was Wednesday, what comes next is an absence
Of all the things we've seen that are not pretty.
The child who ran first to her aid said
That she smiled, saying, "Peter, I've never felt so carefree

Than at this moment." (Peter wasn't his name.)
She just blinked like a bare
Light bulb going to sepia above its chain and string.
You know, A., for all of us it's going to be whatever breezy
Thing comes after Wednesday.
What comes after *A? B!* Then, *C*. But *A*

Is *C!* There are no mysteries.
Just play. I love you, B! *C! A!*
But what comes after Wednesday?
I'd like to think that for the old lady in white,
Under the turning trees, it was a sweet cliff-meeting
Of lovers beside a blue-green sea.

*

To be the ambassador
Of all you are to all that is not you!
CONRAD AIKEN

Why did they whip poor Will? Why? And, then,
You giggled! A., you're just a boy of eleven,
Stunned by what—a revolver emptying itself in the steamy
Morning, in Savannah. WHIP? POOR? WILL? *A dollhouse!*
And how you loved that other orphan: Edgar Poe
Wearing a shawl, coughing while

Sweeping snow off a balcony in Baltimore.
What could we possibly tell him? That there's
Not a single, clandestine cliff-meeting of lovers
In any recent poem of mine, or my contemporaries.
What a loss! I saw it often: their cloaks
Turning in the wind, he turns to kiss her, there is

The blue-green, also-turning sea just beyond them.
Peppermints, here! Get your seltzer and peppermints, here!
But, seriously, do we see Edgar Poe, say, warming his
Fingers in the hot, white jet of a tea-kettle. Do we?
Yes. No.
And also the lovers on the cliffs. A detail. A kiss?

So, you packed the dolls, looked away from the hanging
Gardens of Savannah. Looked away from two pine
Coffins jumping on the flat-bed of a black wagon.
Ruffled a little! You looked away! I've put it
Off until now, but, A.,
They no longer read your poems.

But you said that
You would *stand back*. And so they sent you
Everything through the mails. Prizes, prizes!
Sigmund Freud kept your novel on his desk.
Yellow-book, decadent—the Nazis burned it.
Freud said, "It's a masterpiece. He's a genius."

And, now, they would forget you! In the greater circle . . .
The sheriff that hot morning
In Savannah questioned you, again and again,
About the killings. You told the truth.
And he turned away from you, disgusted with
Your details: the eyes

And mouths of paisley dolls. The temperature. The truth is—
No one reads you, except perhaps,
In Bosschère's hard, snowy country, Finland, and
In Suffolk County, Massachusetts. Bosschère, Poe and
You—what do we do with the orphans?
The orphans who know other orphans?

Trot, trot to Boston. Trot, trot to Lynn!
Indian-pipe, cider, the black swing in the orchard.
You did like New England. But what did we
Do with the orphans—we made them the childless
Ambassadors to a promise that they may remain, forever,
Children! And we never called them back again! Trot, *trot* . . .

To London, Finland, France, and, then, London again.
We give you your Pulitzer with gin.
Did you . . .
Did you have a hatred of women? (You always did
Love the rain.) Our mothers kept us scrubbed, and red,
And crying so that they might remember us just as we

Were when we were introduced to them! Can you blame them?
Try to see her the night before with an Egyptian cigarette
Beside the coffee stains. The government of children is
Left to women. All the Fathers leaving us from the very
                                                                    beginning.
King Henry constantly leaving both the children and the
                                                                    women.
I wrote my first poem when I was eleven. I can still say it.

It wanted to have a line in it that went: *Bang-bang! Bang-bang!*
Not a revolver. Not distant cannons. But thunder on the river.
It didn't work. I'd still like to use the line, somehow.
It's the way of the world that we
Have forgotten our subject, two orphan-poets,
Bosschère and Poe. *The killings.* But who'll tell them.

It was Mother and Father, and the *garden!*
An old story. I, once, wrote that the heads of two
Bald priests could be seen like the buttocks
Of lovers fleeing into the trees. Two coffins
Out in rain. *Bang-bang! Bang-bang!* Cheer up, A.,
For it did rain, the clouds opened, floods came, and *then,*

                                                        more rain.

WINTER WOODS

after *the murals and bottles of Dina Yellen*

The new for us is the last thing our worlds
Have forgotten, brought back by someone, not
Out of necessity, but
Out of the *otherness* of invention which has an unforgiving
Mother, and no father.

The dreams you would have as a girl when you would sweat
And then wake, screaming. What you saw:
The white umbrella,
A primitive mural on a cave wall in woods in Sweden,
Votive tablets, the ancient Oseberg bucket,
The Sumer Warka Head with its pitch-black, feminine mouth,
And silver libation cups. Also, the vermilion ladder, lotus
With water at the middle: its six petals, each
A syllable! And, once, in the afternoon,
A bull's genitals beside broken chalk pencils.

The terracotta and indigo flowers that climb as rope
Up your bottles. The bottles, a clay that's dark as basalt.
The serpentine mural that is larches in winter.
The other mural
Is a procession of animals without human companions:
The mouth of the fox holds an onion that is red like apples!
Roping up the bottles is the viscera of a dead oarsman.
At the wings, a little of the blue of the Mediterranean!

A November night at your studio in the marshlands
Of Vermont: the kilns outside glow against the pines, there
Is lime around the ovens running to snow:
You remember as a child looking
Past the isinglass window of a woodstove to where you saw

A sun, the sun that the Aztec poet described as having one
Flower which is black! Black like Paul Klee's *Moon Flowers*
In a munitions-underground the Nazis built as
An art treasure for a new order of things—
The Nazis who may someday be forgotten, who then will be
Brought back again by someone, not out of necessity, but
Out of a longing for an otherness which will have no mother,

And an unforgiving father.

THOMAS HARDY

The first morning after anyone's death, is it important
To know that fields are wet, that the governess is
Naked but with a scarf still covering her head, that
She's sitting on a gardener who's wearing
Just a blue shirt, or that he's sitting on a chair in the kitchen.
They look like they are rowing while instead outside in the mist
Two boats are passing on the river, the gardener's mouth
Is opening:

A white, screaming bird lifts off the river into the trees,
Flies a short distance and is joined
By a second bird, but then as if to destroy everything
The two white birds are met by a third. *The night
Always fails.* The cows are all now standing in the barns.
You can hear the milk as it drills into wooden pails.

THE RED FIDDLE IN THE MOON PARLOR

1.

You remember the straw hat Melé filled with icy, natal plums
As you sat on a low balcony in Nogales. Now you are
Driving the old truck
Out of Phoenix and in just ten minutes you'll be sitting
On a stool in the open, tin parlors milking cows.

You are seventeen. You call yourself the Sonoran. And Melé
Will be seventeen on Christmas Day. You both believe
That she's pregnant. This dirt road runs along a dry wash.
And out across the desert
The smoke trees puff-up among the indigo, agave scrub—
She embarrassed you, at dawn, at that abandoned
Railway station in the Sierra Madre:

The boarded windows with faded handbills and a single bell
Working out in the hills. An old toothless woman sat beside
You on a bench, her scarf had a dead locust on it, and
Melé began to undress, covering her breasts with
The sombrero she had made from the dry head of a sunflower—
She dropped her skirt and stepped
Into a large rain barrel. She sank in the water with just her
Yellow curls like fallen aspen leaves on the surface.

2.

Two hours of daylight left and then twelve
Hours of night, for fourteen hours you will sit
On the milking stool and tug at
Your lovely cows that listen through the night
While you recite to them two pages of Chekov you've
Translated. You ask them if this time
You've got it just right? Their teats are peach-colored, rough
Like garnet-sheets.

Melé was put on a bus for Oregon, and after a month
She still doesn't write! A hundred and eleven
Cows on a desert farm: your thumb over your little finger,
Both under the palm, and the three remaining fingers
Are, you say, a rusty trident drawing down, stretching
The teats, the yellow milk filling the pails
Until dawn.

Under the black sky with its patch of stars you've named
The cows: *Boötes, Swan, Charles's Wain,*
Orion and *Mons.* You tell these girls
That soon they can eat the blossoming lupine, phlox and
The willow-orchids by the artesian-pond. Two other
                                        workers outside
The open barn are playing ball with a coyote-melon
And they laugh at you: long hair, thick glasses, *la barba negra,*

And your poems. You drink tequila
In the raw milk to keep going. You say you can ignore
The black widow spider who nests in the corner of the barn,
Beside the bales; you have named her *Obsidian.* The red fiddle
On her stomach, you tell her, is worthy
Of Chagall.

3.

When it rains at night into the open barn
Beside the palms
You sing in a canvas poncho to your cows.
Melé's name you've changed to *Verbena.*
Not a word from Verbena in two months.
You've said that you were going back to the Sierra Madre
To find an old woman with a pearl-white insect on her scarf,
To ask her what she remembered of Melé's bath.
Could she describe the girl's shoulders, her legs?

Was there a moon? Was the girl's name
Known to anyone? Did the dish
Run away with the spoon? You laugh!

Again you change Verbena's name, this time to *Cenzina*. But
                                                          then
Back to *Verbena* again. She finally wrote from Portland
Saying you were the father of a little girl. Asking if you
Would like to name her?
You settled on *Beth*. Just Beth!
You said once the boss at the farm took
A photo of Melé and you in the barn. You saw it
And said, "Virgin with child." A manger in the desert!
Bethlehem? Beth.
I preferred: Cholla or Dalea! We laughed.

And now you're gone. Your cows must be giving vinegar.
The old truck you probably abandoned somewhere
In the Dakotas. You might have gone to Oregon,
Or Canada. You said that one day you would turn up
Missing. Not to worry.

You're probably a dishwasher. The dish
And the spoon, or a cold night with stars walking back
To your room must remind you
Of your girls in their barn. I remember you

Sitting on the milking stool, the broken laces
Of your shoes. And how you would
Put a little salt on your tongue, swallowing tequila
And then grinning, drink straight from the teat
Of Orion or Boötes. You said, "Only a king may kill a king."

Melé wrote! I opened her letter in the evening—
She said you lived together
For three weeks, the only work you found
Was in a slaughterhouse. And you were still

Naming animals.
You walked them from the trains under the stars
And into a room with chutes.

That your name was now *Joe*. Just Joe.
That you accused Melé of being unfaithful. That you finally
Stopped naming animals!

You couldn't eat. You were certain the government
Was grinding cattle bones into our milk.
You left her a note: *I am going to another country*.
You went to Canada. Climbed stairs
To the roof of a tall building . . .

Melé said you would drink her breast milk. That
Each evening you brought the baby a balloon.
She said, "I'm sorry. But, in Canada, under a clear night sky—
Joe heard a little dog laugh. Joe jumped

Over the moon."

A LAMB, A WOOLEN LAMB

They cut the red threads—
They broke the voice,
*   but it is singing*
Together with us,
Together under the flags,
It rises, your voice
*   of blood and song.*
                            VICTOR JARA

The blood complicates your hair, dark sienna and matted
Like the roofs of hillside huts . . . your strong nose,
And on the shirt over your corpse there's an insect:
A live, giant lacewing: one stilled lime-green wing,
And the other tipped wing is red, three of its legs lifted
Up out of the blood on your chest. Your chest, the
Open pits . . . dark mules with ore walking a narrow
Cliff-road that winds down to the mines past the cool sheds.

In your hand there's a bullet, a bit of waxed string.
Along the coast of Mexico on the day of your death
A storm picked up a window box of tall roses
And drove them, individually, four inches into
An adobe wall in a village two miles inland, the
Great heads of these flowers were not hurt.
They live in this shaded wall that's constantly watered.
Like governments, death can decorate the dead: ice-green,
Lime-green and red. *Victor,*

Your songs are coal! And Chile sleeps the stubborn sleep
Of the horizontal rose
In its baked, day-white, vertical bed.

ELEGY TO THE SIOUX

The vase was made of clay
With spines of straw
For strength. The sun-baked vase
Soaked in a deep blue dye for days. The events in this wilderness,
Portrayed in the round of the vase,

Depend on shades of indigo against
The masked areas of the clay, a flat pearl color
To detail the big sky and snow . . .

This Montana field in winter is not sorrowful: A bugle skips
                                        through notes:
We view it all somehow from the center of the field
And there are scattered groups of cavalry. Some of these
Men were seasoned by civil war. Their caps are blue.
Their canteens are frozen. The horses shake their heads
Bothered by the beads of ice, the needles of ice
Forming at both sides of their great anvil heads.

The long blue cloaks of the officers fall over the haunches
Of the horses. The ammunition wagons
Beside the woods are blurred by the snowy weather . . .

Beyond the wagons, further even, into the woods
There is a sloping stream bed. This is
The dark side of the vase which is often misunderstood.
From here through the bare trees there's
A strange sight to be seen at the very middle of the field:

A valet is holding a bowl of cherries—archetype and rubric,
A general with white hair eats the fruit while introducing its
                                        color
Which will flow through the woods in early December.
An Indian woman came under dark clouds to give birth,
                                        unattended

In the deep wash inside the woods. She knew the weather

Could turn, and staked the tips of two rooted spruce trees
To the earth to make a roof.
The deerskin of her robe is in her mouth. Her legs spread,
Her feet are tied up in the roof of darkening spruce. *No stars
Show through!* But on the vase that belonged to a President
There are countless stars above the soldiers' campfires . . .

With rawhide her feet are tied high in the spruce
And her left hand is left loose as if she were about
To ride a wild stallion
                              to its conclusion in a box canyon.

President Grant drinks bourbon from his boot. The Sioux
Cough in their blankets . . .

It snowed an hour more, and then the moon appeared. The
                                                  unborn infant,
Almost out on the forest floor, buckled and lodged. It died.
Its mother died. Just before she closed her eyes
She rubbed snow up and down the inside of her bare thighs.

In the near field an idle, stylish horse raised one leg
To make a perfect right angle. Just then a ghost of snow formed
Over the tents of the soldiers,

It blows past the stylish, gray horse,
Unstopped it moves through woods, up the stream bed
And passes into the crude spruce shelter, into the raw open
Woman, her legs raised into sky—
Naked house of snow and ice! This gust of wind

Spent the night within the woman. At sunrise, it left her mouth
Tearing out trees, keeping the owls from sleep; it was angry now
And into the field it spilled, into the bivouac of pony-soldiers

Who turned to the south, who turned back to the woods, who
                                                        became

Still. Blue all over! If there is snow still unspooling in the
                                                        mountains
Then there is time yet for the President to get his Indian vase
And to fill it with bourbon from his boot and to put flowers into
                                                        it:
The flowers die in a window that looks out on a cherry tree
Which heavy with fruit drops a branch:

                    torn to its very heartwood
By the red clusters of fruit, the branch fell
Like her leg and foot
Out of the big sky into Montana . . .

                                        For Dave Smith

ELIZABETH'S WAR WITH THE CHRISTMAS BEAR: 1601

For Paul Zimmer

The bears are kept by hundreds within fences, are fed cracked
Eggs; the weakest are
Slaughtered and fed to the others after being scented
With the blood of deer brought to the pastures by Elizabeth's
Men—the blood spills from deep pails with bottoms of slate.

The balding Queen had bear-gardens in London and in the
                                                        country.
The bear is baited: the nostrils
Are blown full with pepper, the Irish wolf dogs
Are starved, then, emptied, made crazy with fermented barley;

And the bear's hind leg is chained to a stake, the bear
Is blinded and whipped, kneeling in his own blood and slaver,
                                                        he is
Almost instantly worried by the dogs. At the very moment that
Elizabeth took Essex's head, a giant brown bear
Stood in the gardens with dogs hanging from his fur . . .
He took away the sun, took
A wolfhound in his mouth and tossed it into
The white lap of Elizabeth I—arrows and staves rained

On his chest, and standing, he, then, stood even taller, seeing
Into the Queen's private boxes—he grinned into her battered
                                                        eggshell face.
Another volley of arrows and poles, and opening his mouth he
                                                        showered
Blood all over Elizabeth and her Privy Council.

The very next evening, a cool evening, the Queen demanded
13 bears and the justice of 113 dogs: She slept

All that Sunday night and much of the next morning.
Some said she was guilty of *this* and *that*.
The Protestant Queen gave the defeated bear
A grave in a Catholic cemetery. The marker said:
Peter, a Solstice Bear, a gift of the Tsarevitch to Elizabeth.

After a long winter she had the grave opened. The bear's
          skeleton
Was cleared with lye, she placed it at her bedside,
Put a candle inside behind the sockets of the eyes, and, then
She spoke to it:

You were a Christmas bear—behind your eyes
I see the walls of a snow cave where you are a cub still smelling
Of your mother's blood which has dried in your hair; you have
Troubled a Queen who was afraid when seated in *shade* which,
          standing,

You had created! A Queen who often wakes with a dream of
          you at night—
Now, you'll stand by my bed in your long white bones; alone,
          you
Will frighten away at night all visions of bear, and all day
You will be in this cold room—your constant grin,
You'll stand in the long, white prodigy of your bones, and you
          are,
Every inch of you, a terrible vision, not bear, but virgin!

THE ARS POETICA OF SØREN KIERKEGAARD

For William Keens

I could not have built my community

Without *the other*. I will not acknowledge that
The other is a mob of constellations (*Cygnus*
Who is The Swan; *Draco,* The Dragon; and *Boötes*),
They are now milling down into the conifers along the water.
They are not *the other*. Perhaps, it is

The paddle boat bleaching out in our pasture in
The blue cornflowers. Sister Luther dries stalks
Of sunflowers out there in its lamp-room, then
They are twisted and dressed into giant dolls . . .
There was
A wild, red-haired ploughman, and the wife of a
Potato farmer in a white dress, she had a knife
In one hand and in the other, a fish head . . .
All of Sister Luther's dolls are copied from life.
Brother Thomas thought that they were best described as
Copied from the dead. They were

Life-size, dreadful, astonishing. Sister Luther
Was clever: she grew a variegated arrow-vine
Among the steps of the paddle wheel so that it
Presented to the eye an illusion of actually dappled,
Churning water. I am not a poet, but

When I was younger I could attach my mind to
A clap of thunder as it rolled through our valley
And emptied out over the lake and its glacier.
It was a thrill like coasting on the children's
Waxed toboggan, in summer, as it rushed down

The dry stream beds over mica flows and the rounded
Glacial stones. *The other* isn't my community of which
All of the others are absent . . .

It is a figure worthy of being another
Of Sister Luther's parched, clothed sunflowers.
It is seen in the evening when the cuckoo begins
Screaming. The figure is clearly me rising
Out of the lake, a phantom dressed in white
With a sack-sling of bean seeds by my side,
Scattering the seed from side to side
Over the dark water. I am wearing a straw hat
With a great brim made of live bees and lacewings,
For shoes I am wearing curved staves
From a rain barrel. I am clean-shaven.
Sowing seeds. I promised my wife that
I would crowd her grave with bean flowers.
She drowned out there near the black rocks.

When the lightening touches the village below me
I remember the scene: she
Just slid into the water wearing her
Lavender dress . . . she did it to cool herself
I guessed. We just rowed about in that spot
Dragging the bottom with a rope tied to an iron-share
That had snapped the day before in the garden.

In spring, the goatherd comes up here from the village,
And, just a boy, he doesn't fear me! He will even tell
Me, gently, that the villagers insist that there *never*
Were others in my community! Thirty years ago, he says,
They were expected to travel here from *Zurich*
But, the goatherd says, they never did: He admits
That my wife was among them. He becomes angry
With me and says, "This is stupid, old man! Come and
Live with my sisters and me in the village." Then,

I begin to sob, saying, "You are God's favorite, goatherd!
Do you not sing to your sheep? We all live solitary lives.
I must go now

And scatter seeds over my wife. This breeze
Will make it difficult.
I hear thunder in the distance. Perhaps, it is
The heavy shimmering jubilee-wagons of my community coming
For me? Poor goatherd, if you die up here

In the mountains, in springtime,
Only I will remember
Everything about you. And campion with daisies
Will grow over your grave
Like the undivided memory
Of something simple, that belonged to another,

That you had promised to save."

AUBADE OF THE SINGER AND
SABOTEUR, MARIE TRISTE: 1941

In the twenties, I would visit Dachau often with my brother.
There was then an artists' colony outside the Ingolstadt Woods
And these estates had a meadow filled
With the hazy blood-campion, sumac and the delicate yellow
                                                    cinquefoil.
At the left of the meadow there was a fast stream and pond, and
Along the stream, the six lodges and the oak Dachau Hall where
Meals were held and the evening concerts. In winter, the Hall
Was a hostel for hunters, and the violinists who were the first
Of the colony to arrive in spring would spend three days
Scouring the deer blood off the floors, tables, walls and sinks.
They would rub myrtle leaves into the wood to get out the stink!

The railway from Munich to Ingolstadt would deposit us by
The gold water-tower and my brother, Charles, and I would cut
Across two fields to the pastures behind Dachau Hall. Once,
Crossing these fields, Charles, who had been drinking warm

                                                    beer
Since morning, stopped, and crouching low in the white chicory
And lupine found a single, reddish touch-me-not which is rare
Here in the mountains. A young surgeon, Charles assumed his
Condescending tone, and began by saying, "Now, little sister,

This flower has no perfume—what you smell is not your
Brother's breath either, but the yeast-sheds of the brewery just

                                                    over
That hill. This uncommon flower can grow to an enormous

                                                    height
If planted in water. It is a succulent annual. Its private
Appointments are oval and its nodding blossom takes its weight
From pods with crimson threadlike supports." With his bony

                                                    fingers

He began to force open the flower. *I blushed*. He said, "It is
A devoted, sexual flower. Its tough, meatlike labia protrude
Until autumn and then shrivel; this adult flower
If disturbed explodes *into a small yellow rain like*
That fawn we watched urinating on the hawthorn just last
                                                    August."

Charles was only two years younger but could be a wicked
                                                    fellow.
Once, on our first day at the colony, at midnight, he was
Discovered nude and bathing in the pond with a cellist. She was
The only cellist, and for that week, Charles was their only
                                                    doctor.
So neither was banished. But neither was spoken to except
For rehearsals and in illness. There is a short bridge passage
In a Scriabin sonata that reminds me of the bursting touch-me-
                                                    nots,
That remind me, also, of Heisdt-Bridge *itself,* in Poland! We
                                                    blew
It up in October. I had primed the packages of glycerin,
                                                    kieselguhr,
Woodmeal and chalk. We curbed the explosives with sulphur.
I sat in primrose and sorrel with the plunger-box and at four
                                                    o'clock
Up went the munitions shipment from Munich to Warsaw.
                                                    Those thin
Crimson supports of the flower tossed up like the sunburned
                                                    arms
Of the pianist Mark Meichnik, arriving at his favorite E-flat
Major chord; and I guess that whenever a train or warehouse
                                                    went
Four-ways-to-market right before my eyes, I thought
Of that large moment of Schumann's. The morning
After Heisdt-Bridge I was captured and Charles

Was shot.

I was at Dachau by the weekend. They have kept me in
A small cell. A young Lieutenant tortured me all that first night.
Knowing I was a singer they asked me to perform
For the Commandant early the next week.
By then I was able to stand again, but my Nazi inquisitor
Had for an hour touched live wires to me while holding
Me in a shallow ice bath. I had been
Made into a tenor voice! The Commandant's wife dismissed me
After just a few notes. As I was tortured I forced myself
To dwell on the adult life of the touch-me-not, that fawn in
Hawthorn and my brother's drunken anatomy lesson that
                                                        showed
No skill at all there in the silver meadow. I was probably
Stupid not to have fallen unconscious. When I was
Ordered out of the parlor by the Nazi bitch, I did, for the first

Time in two years, cry aloud. I think it was for my voice that
I cried so badly. The guards laughed, returning me to my cell.
My cell has a bench, a pail and a wire brush. Every two days
Without warning the hose comes alive with water, moving
                                                        through
The space like a snake. Sometimes it wakes me about the face
                                                        and legs.
I have lost so much weight that I can sleep comfortably
On the pine bench. I watch shadows in the cell become,
At night, the masquerade dance in the woodcut by Hans
                                                Burgkmair:

Its bird shapes, that procession of *men* threading the dance,
And *Maximilian I* greeting them as they twist past the banquet
                                                        tables.
My inquisitor, all that night in the chamber, commanding me
To sing, to sing!

When they fire the ovens out beside the pastures it is like
A giant catching his breath. And then there is the silence

Of the trucks with just their murmuring engines. My delusions:
A sound like my brother's cellist, at this early hour, opening
The morning with difficult arm exercises; he said that she would
Play for him naked and until he became jealous. Then I would
Say, "Oh, Charles!" He'd laugh.

My favorite pastime has become the imaginary destruction of
                                                                    flowers.
I hear their screams. They bleed onto the floor of my cell. I scrub
Afterwards sometimes for hours. I play the violin also. And I
                                                                    scrub
The wall where a *Bürgermeister* opened the artery of a doe that
He had shot just outside the window.
Later, the *Bürgermeister's* favorite butcher making venison
                                                                    flanks
Into roasts, how he sawed at the large femur of the deer
Like the cellist waking with her instrument, their right arms
Are beautiful with white muscles;
The butcher and the cellist died, here, admiring the noxious
Blue crystals on the floors of the gas-chamber: the way,

At first, they darken to indigo and like smoke
Climb over your ankles, reaching your waist—
You fall naked as into the field that is with a breeze turning
All its wildflowers, bladder-campion and myrtle, into
A melody of just three staves written for four voices:

Slaughter and music,
Two of the old miracles. They were not my choices.

THE SIBLINGS' WOODCUT: *Dementia Praecox*

In the deep chocolate shade of the woodcut
I discovered the cloaks of flown birds—
The animals had a garden party without us.
A notebook, bound in hickory boards, lists all
The new offspring of diminutive mule deer, bobcat

And crow. The notebook has spilled into the furrowing
Windy grass of the lawn. A fox scolds the squirrels.
The old moles will be the last to find their way,
Their dead reckoning
Back into the spacious birch forest . . . my father

Is in London,
Soap has dried in his shaving mug, the soft
Bristles of the brush are like
Burnt sugar with cream, the mixed coloring
Of badgers! Robin Hood used the hair of badgers

To weight the green wood of an arrow.
On my father's steamships the young of badgers
Are shipped in crates to France or Spain.
Have you ever measured distances by sound;
If the steam from a ship's whistle is seen
And, say, ten seconds elapse before the sound
Is heard by you again, then *she* is just
Two miles off—entering a fog bank, I think! Mother is
Dead. She taught me the night signals of the Cunard Line:

There are three orange lights, one forward, one aft,
One amidships; simultaneous roman candles
Burst above us, throwing six gold balls across the stern—
A green Costen light follows a red star that burns
For twelve seconds in its maiden flight. . . .

The influence of the moon, I'm sorry,
Is not detailed in the thin woodcut. Our cat, a large

Russian Blue, circles this memory of childhood, in which
I thought to ask Grandmother if she understood

The shyness of animals. She peered
Into the scene and spoke aloud: *There will be a bitter frost,*
And hounds below a full moon! She stopped? I was
Hurt, I thought she didn't want to answer. Then I heard:

The bountiful shyness of animals is winter news,
At liberty like rusty worms in an armful of rusty apples.
Who do you think it is they are shy of?

I looked out of the woodcut
And up through the soft platinum hair
Of her nostrils which turned into a willow

Peacefully nudging another willow!
Again, I understood I was forbidden to tell anyone
What I had witnessed, what I had just construed. . . .

Of course, Grandmother and my little sister, Maud,
Already knew. . . .
Maud says they will someday tell me too. Is it
Us the animals fear? Or is it
My mother's woodcut
With open-air butchers at narrow, crudely built tables,
In an autumn clearing, in sainted Sherwood Forest?

From all directions the celebrated, large-hearted
Archers of Old England
Drag the corpses of stag, fox,
Boar, quail, raven, and across

The rounded, sagging shoulders of Robin Hood is the
Sheriff's spring calf—
Its fawn neck has the outlaw's long arrow in it!

THE GREAT WALL OF CHINA

Below my turret the spotted cows plough through the circuit
Of their day, a passage from meadow to brook
To willows to the recognition of a distant
Brilliantly lit parlor with straw in its high lofts . . .
Cows come at us like sour, ponderous kittens,
With empty attention, not yet weaned
From the lacunae of a milk-pitcher that's beaded

With sweat. The blue wheel of cheese
Has short white hairs growing on it.
I was fifty-three years of age, yesterday.
I'm one of four palace sentries transferred to the Wall
Near the Black Desert but
East of it beside the mariposa-tiers of the green Husi Gorge.
It was said that I had knowledge of three of the Dowager's
virgins.

A masked white-and-black kitten is asleep in my lap,
I would not disturb its falling through dreams, not even
If barbarians came rattling and huffing over the horizon:
They too would be dreaming, but of the obese Dowager's
Body-net of sapphires and rubies!

There have been years of fasting without a carnival!

My great cloak shields my eyes like a wing, rain suddenly
Traversing the countryside. By the brook, nevertheless,
Two lovers embrace, you cannot
Draw a geometer's straight line between them
For they have eclipsed
One another with just such an axiom.
Pine needles stick to their glistening skin. She holds him back:
Saying:

It's your root husband we center on, but my root is strong also
A vine on which are strung the sleeping pods of our unborn, all
                                                    of them!
The children stretch from me to that sagging ridgepole . . .
And there is a shadow like a weight
In our unmade bed. An aspect

Of the mother must be concealed from us; that aspect
Emerges, after much thought, in the lovers she selects for us.
I have listened
Innocently from my battlement to a young couple speaking,
In repose, as the rain slowed, having messed the impression
Of a large basket, left by the lovers in the soft rusty needles
Of what cannot last. The cows in their circles are weighted
                                                    against us!
The ultimate, physical harmony
Of lovers is pain softened into the oblivion of music. . . .
My three kittens dance foolishly to my whittled pipe of
                                                    mahogany.

Often, with a delicate pin, I take a seed from an apple. But only
With the greed
Of a newborn feeding at a breast
Can we pluck from the seed, a buffed
Red apple that's cross-stitched with gold

And sweeter
Than the laughter of any life to come. . . .

NORMAN DUBIE was born in Barre, Vermont, in April 1945. His poems have appeared in many magazines including *The Paris Review, The New Yorker, The American Poetry Review, Antaeus,* and *Poetry.* For his work, he has won The Bess Hokin Award of *Poetry,* and a fellowship from The John Simon Guggenheim Memorial Foundation. He lives in Tempe, Arizona, with his wife, the poet Pamela Stewart, and their daughter, Hannah. Mr. Dubie is a member of the English Department at Arizona State University.